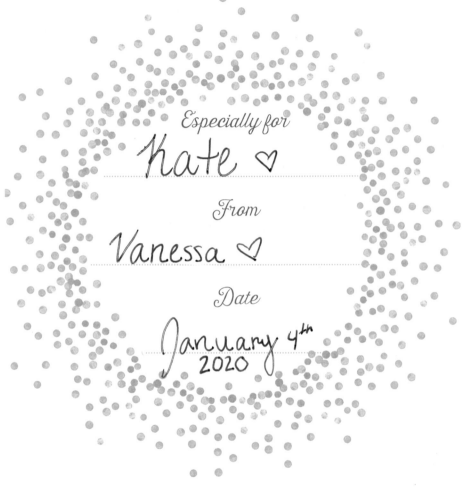

Especially for

Kate ♡

From

Vanessa ♡

Date

January 4ᵗʰ
2020

Choosing
REAL

A Devotional
Thought Journal

Bekah Jane Pogue

Choosing
REAL

A Devotional
Thought Journal

SHILOH RUN PRESS
An Imprint of Barbour Publishing, Inc.

Published in association with The Blythe Daniel Agency, P.O. Box 64197, Colorado Springs, CO 80962-4197.

Published by Shiloh Run Press, an imprint of Barbour Publishing, Inc., 1810 Barbour Drive, Uhrichsville, Ohio 44683, www.shilohrunpress.com

Our mission is to inspire the world with the life-changing message of the Bible.

ecpa Member of the
Evangelical Christian
Publishers Association

Printed in China.

An Invitation to
Choose REAL

How I wish I could plop you on my couch with an iced chai in one hand and a ginormous brownie in the other to see your eyes and whisper this: "You, my friend, you don't have to work so hard. You don't have to host the party and put out your best and cook for the masses. You don't have to strive to perform, because God is already in it. He is present right this very minute. He is using every aspect of the unplanned as an invitation for you to pause and enjoy Him first. Just you and your Father. He's offering space to meet. To get to know you. He wants to listen to your dreams and fears, to hold your hand and surprise you in out-of-the-box ways. He's inviting you to celebrate how *His* manifestations may look different than *your* expectations.

How will you choose to respond?

This is where choosing Real began for me. And choosing Real can begin here for you too.

I pray this journal will help You to get real with Jesus. And I hope you accept my invitation to journey with me as we look at how He is present in the oh-so-normal stuff. God longs for us to experience Him today. *Right now.* At work, in the grocery aisle, surrounded by people who require attention, or wherever life throws curve balls. When I'm tempted to plan my days to resemble an epic party, I'm choosing to grasp, laugh over, cling to, cry about, and celebrate just how real He truly is.

And from here, all of life is breathed and exhaled.

Walk alongside me, and choose REAL today.

~ Bekah

1/5/2020

You make known to me the path of life; you will fill me with joy in your presence, with eternal pleasures at your right hand.

PSALM 16:11 NIV

This verse brings me so much peace in a time where I feel very little. Time and time again you have proven that your timing is best and better than anything I could plan myself. I truthfully feel uneasy and unsure about so many things. Lord, help me to continually write this verse on my heart. You make known to me my path, and you fill me with joy!! Keep my focus on You, your Kingdom, and your work. My word for 2020 is FOCUS, so help me do just that.

God is using every aspect of the unplanned as an invitation for you to pause and enjoy Him first. Just you and your Father. He's offering space to meet. To get to know you.

How might you quiet your heart and mind today and just steep yourself in the heavenly Father's beautiful presence?

For I know the thoughts that I think toward you,
says the LORD, thoughts of peace and not of evil,
to give you a future and a hope.

JEREMIAH **29:11** NKJV

God wants to listen to your dreams and fears, to hold your hand and surprise you in out-of-the-box ways. He's inviting you to celebrate how *His* manifestations may look different from *your* expectations.

How is God surprising you in an "out-of-the-box" way?

....

....

....

....

....

....

....

....

....

....

....

....

....

....

....

....

....

....

....

....

Blessed is the nation whose God is the LORD,
the people he chose for his inheritance.

PSALM 33:12 NIV

Only when my head connects to my heart and I know with
every fiber in me that Jesus is already here and chooses me,
then, and only then, can I move forward.

*What does it look like to respond to Jesus' invitation
for a genuine relationship with Him?*

Let me hear in the morning of your steadfast love,
for in you I trust. Make me know the way
I should go, for to you I lift up my soul.

PSALM 143:8 ESV

What if we let God lay out the dreams He has placed within us, since before time, in the order He knows best? What if we choose to know He is weaving passion and pain and grace so personally together that it *has* to be journeyed with Him to appreciate His peace all the more?

How are you saying yes?

....

....

....

....

....

....

....

....

....

....

....

....

....

....

....

....

....

....

....

....

Therefore the LORD waits to be gracious to you, and therefore he exalts himself to show mercy to you. For the LORD is a God of justice; blessed are all those who wait for him.

ISAIAH **30:18** ESV

God's Spirit beckons, presenting a choice to create my own
path, even under the mask of faith—or recognize Him as
The Inviter, The One Who Has Already Shown Up.

How is God inviting you?

....

....

....

....

....

....

....

....

....

....

....

....

....

....

....

....

....

....

....

"If you then, being evil, know how to give good gifts to your children, how much more will your Father who is in heaven give good things to those who ask Him!"

MATTHEW 7:11 NKJV

God is a giver of good gifts, but I have to trust He knows *when* and *how* and *why* to give them. And that He remains constantly Real even when gifts are taken away.

How are you choosing to see how Real God is in your circumstances, emotions, and relationships?

....

....

....

....

....

....

....

....

....

....

....

....

....

....

....

....

....

....

*"Ask, and it will be given to you; seek,
and you will find; knock, and it will be opened to you."*

MATTHEW 7:7 NKJV

....
....
....
....
....
....
....
....
....
....
....
....
....
....
....
....
....
....

When Jesus invites, when He shows up and knocks gently, when He whispers through classmates and coworkers, co-op moms and crazy calendars, we have the choice to accept and walk through the door with Him or to continue assuming the main role of inviter.

When we know how it feels to be invited in, why do we so often refuse these invitations and go about our way, hoping He'll ask later when we're less busy?

....

....

....

....

....

....

....

....

....

....

....

....

....

....

....

....

"Come, all you who are thirsty, come to the waters;
and you who have no money, come, buy and eat!
Come, buy wine and milk without money and without cost.
Why spend money on what is not bread, and your labor
on what does not satisfy? Listen, listen to me, and eat
what is good, and you will delight in the richest of fare."

ISAIAH 55:1–2 NIV

God starts with an invitation, an offering of Himself. On the cross, Jesus invited me to follow. And since then, His invitations haven't ceased. No wonder He starts by meeting me where I am in my current season.

How is God meeting you right now in this very moment?

....

....

....

....

....

....

....

....

....

....

....

....

....

....

....

....

....

....

"Come, follow me," Jesus said.

MATTHEW 4:19 NIV

....
....
....
....
....
....
....
....
....
....
....
....
....
....
....
....
....
....
....
....

An invitation is by far the most beautiful expression of love and grace. It requires no work on my part, other than acceptance. God's invitation includes all of life, every dark corner and every vibrant, celebratory space.

When Jesus says, "Come," how do you typically respond?

....

....

....

....

....

....

....

....

....

....

....

....

....

....

....

....

....

....

....

"Choose this day whom you will serve. . . .
As for me and my house, we will serve the LORD."

JOSHUA **24:15** ESV

....

....

....

....

....

....

....

....

....

....

....

....

....

....

....

....

....

....

Real life begs the invitation to follow Jesus. In each season of faith, I have a choice to agree that He knows best and trust His perspective, or to do things on my own. By following Him into the real stuff, the true grit, He transforms the tiniest of details and the darkest of valleys, drawing me closer to His heart.

He holds out His hand and invites us to follow. Dance parties included. Will you RSVP to Jesus' invitation with an intentional yes?

....

....

....

....

....

....

....

....

....

....

....

....

....

....

....

....

....

*He got up and rebuked the wind and the raging waters;
the storm subsided, and all was calm.*

LUKE 8:24 NIV

....
....
....
....
....
....
....
....
....
....
....
....
....
....
....
....
....
....

To rest means to be filled up by the One who enjoys us right in the middle of the rush. Authentic rest emulates our Father; it's turning my mind and heart to settle into a cozy rhythm that models Him, even if a million dishes are flying about the kitchen.

What do you think of when you hear the word **rest**?

....

....

....

....

....

....

....

....

....

....

....

....

....

....

....

....

....

....

"Come to Me, all you who labor and are heavy laden, and I will give you rest. Take my yoke upon you and learn from Me, for I am gentle and lowly in heart, and you will find rest for your souls. For My yoke is easy and My burden is light."

MATTHEW 11:28–30 NKJV

It's often in pain and waiting room unknowns; it's in suffering and darkness where God wants to offer Himself and bring peace to our minds and spirits, because that's when we desperately need Him. No amount of fast-forwarding or busyness can create enough friction to launch us past needing peace. As long as there are waiting room seasons, we can either respond by wading through the mess or denying it. Enjoying or escaping.

How do you truly know if you have peace?
Where do you notice this in your body?

Do not be anxious about anything, but in everything by prayer and supplication with thanksgiving let your requests me made known to God. And the peace of God, which surpasses all understanding, will guard your hearts and your minds in Christ Jesus.

PHILIPPIANS 4:6–7 ESV

If worry is a symptom of a hurried life, the root issue is control. Somewhere along the journey of growing up, we went from being cared for to taking care of others. We neglected the middle part, where we opt to be cared for by the Soul Nourisher in order to care for others. When I live being filled *first*, care-taking is life-giving, not exhausting.

What does enjoying the journey look like in the rush?
In the busy? In the responsibilities and demands of life?

....

....

....

....

....

....

....

....

....

....

....

....

....

....

....

....

Seek peace and pursue it.

Psalm 34:14 NKJV

....

....

....

....

....

....

....

....

....

....

....

....

....

....

....

....

....

....

....

....

....

....

....

Friends, hear this: Rest is not selfish; it is essential. It is biblical. When fall greets, red leaves blink warnings—not to *physically* stop— but to focus *mind* and *heart* toward Jesus-offering peace.

In what circumstance is your soul craving peace today?

....

....

....

....

....

....

....

....

....

....

....

....

....

....

....

....

....

....

....

....

*You have searched me, LORD, and you know me.
You know when I sit and when I rise; you perceive
my thoughts from afar. You discern my going out and
my lying down; you are familiar with all my ways.*

PSALM 139:1–3 NIV

To embrace rest and inner peace. Serenity *among* the crazy. Isn't that what we desire? Not to cancel life, move to a mountain, and claim stillness, but to really know Jesus' genuine heart, where calm is obtainable in the hustle-bustle of humanity.

What is keeping you from embracing rest?
How will you carve out intentional space for this?

....

....

....

....

....

....

....

....

....

....

....

....

....

....

....

....

....

"My Presence will go with you, and I will give you rest."

EXODUS 33:14 NIV

At our core is the need to be loved, to be enjoyed by God first. I know it sounds obvious, but when I lose myself to God's Spirit, I find my truest self.

What would it look like to rid yourself of the box you believe God has to meet you in, and instead choose to let Him enjoy you for who you are?

....

....

....

....

....

....

....

....

....

....

....

....

....

....

....

....

....

Who can proclaim the mighty acts
of the LORD or fully declare his praise?

PSALM 106:2 NIV

If it's rest we need to live fully, it's the minutes we must enjoy, for those are when God shows up.

What are some simple things that bring you peace in the daily chaos of life? Make a list here.

"The LORD bless you and keep you; the LORD make his face shine on you and be gracious to you; the LORD turn his face toward you and give you peace."

NUMBERS 6:24–26 NIV

You are enjoyed by the Creator. *Just. as. you. are.* And His peace doesn't come when we cancel our calendars and sit alone on a mountain. If it did, I wouldn't be interested in that kind of faith. What I crave is understanding a Creator who crashes into real life in real time through everyday offerings.

Do you sense the heavenly Creator drawing you to rest in His presence even now?

....
....
....
....
....
....
....
....
....
....
....
....
....
....
....
....
....

. . .to bestow on them a crown of beauty instead of ashes, the oil of joy instead of mourning, and a garment of praise instead of a spirit of despair.

Isaiah **61:3** niv

Loss *is* more. It provides a narrowed, stripped-down, beauty-from-ashes, life-from-death perspective. It takes the future I intended, turns it upside down, shakes my goals, and replaces them with Real's plan. Loss pulls away cobwebs from my eyes, clears a dull humming in my ears, and forces me to evaluate what really matters.

Consider a loss that transformed your perspective.
What really matters since that experience?

....

....

....

....

....

....

....

....

....

....

....

....

....

....

....

....

....

....

Weeping may stay for the night,
but rejoicing comes in the morning.

PSALM 30:5 NIV

Loss pulls out the shadowed colors and brings them to vivid light.
It focuses a flashlight on the present, and for that moment,
the present is all to be celebrated and grabbed onto, for beyond
the brilliant light is He who holds eternity. And for this reason,
suffering is stomached, not because it's easy to swallow,
but for the sheer joy at knowing life waits on the other side.

What "in the moment" celebration can you have today?

....

....

....

....

....

....

....

....

....

....

....

....

....

....

....

....

....

*Blessed be the God and Father of our Lord Jesus Christ,
the Father of mercies and God of all comfort.*

2 CORINTHIANS 1:3 NKJV

Even without looking for God, He finds us. In the dark.
Tired. Blank. Sad. And He offers His comfort.

*When have you felt alone and without hope? How did
God comfort when you needed Him most? Take some
time to reflect and thank Him for His nearness.*

....

....

....

....

....

....

....

....

....

....

....

....

....

....

....

....

....

....

....

....

"Behold, I make all things new."

REVELATION 21:5 NKJV

When flower centerpieces wither and die days after a party, we can use the fallen petals and repurpose death into something new. Although a different, unexpected new, this purpose still has beauty. And God does the same. He arranges the fallen petals in our lives to confetti a tablescape for everyday settings, where they hint at memories of what *was* and offer hope for what can *be*.

How have you noticed God bringing
unexpected beauty and purpose from loss?

....

....

....

....

....

....

....

....

....

....

....

....

....

....

....

But I will hope continually,
And will praise You yet more and more.

PSALM 71:14 NKJV

Isn't it easy to assume that if we're embracing change, what follows will be easy? But it's the messiness of transition, the center that builds dependence on Jesus and roots a solid identity. What if we don't have to look back? What if we can have a confident Christ-identity, knowing He is enough in the here and now?

What makes embracing change difficult? Sit with these thoughts and feelings for a bit and then take them to the Father.

....

....

....

....

....

....

....

....

....

....

....

....

....

....

....

....

"Have I not commanded you? Be strong and courageous.
Do not be afraid; do not be discouraged, for the LORD
your God will be with you wherever you go."

JOSHUA 1:9 NIV

Jesus, I'm learning, is near me in emotions. He says, *"I relate. I get it. And as much as you are sad or unsettled, I too have felt that way, and I am bigger than your feelings."* And then He encourages me to depend on Him when I want to lead with my emotions. Feelings hint at my very need to cling closer to the Father, who created them. He fills in the gaps between my independence and dependence, completing my worth in Him.

What does being okay mean to you?
Where do you need permission to not be okay?

....

....

....

....

....

....

....

....

....

....

....

....

....

....

Yet to all who did receive him, to those who believed in his name, he gave the right to become children of God.

JOHN 1:12 NIV

....
....
....
....
....
....
....
....
....
....
....
....
....
....
....
....
....
....

When situations shift, I care less about trying to force authenticity and more about simply depending on a genuine Jesus. When I do, my focus naturally transfers from *me* to *Him*. I find comfort knowing I am *enough*, for the Spirit of the Lord lives inside me. No matter what happens, my identity will not be shaken.

How does claiming a Jesus identity fit as
snug and cozy as your comfy pants?

....

....

....

....

....

....

....

....

....

....

....

....

....

....

....

....

Therefore, if anyone is in Christ, he is a new creation; old things have passed away; behold, all things have become new.

2 CORINTHIANS 5:17 NKJV

When you release control and allow God to be enough, freedom comes—freedom to be present to His work in every detail of your life, trusting He is making all things new. Even in transition.

How does your identity reflect your Maker?

....
....
....
....
....
....
....
....
....
....
....
....
....
....
....
....
....
....

*Your beauty should not come from outward adornment,
such as elaborate hairstyles and the wearing of gold jewelry
or fine clothes. Rather, it should be that of your inner
self, the unfading beauty of a gentle and quiet spirit,
which is of great worth in God's sight.*

1 PETER 3:3–4 NIV

True beauty is letting God be strong when you feel done. Beauty is smiling even when your heart hurts. Beauty is trusting that your worth is solidified in a God of grace who knows your thoughts and fears and sees you giving your best today and wraps you in His embrace and shines a light on your face and declares, "*You. Are. Beautiful.*"

How would you define true beauty?

Charm is deceptive, and beauty is fleeting;
but a woman who fears the LORD is to be praised.

PROVERBS **31:30** NIV

Do you notice and acknowledge how God reflects your created worth when you glance in the mirror? Where you critique your body with scrutiny in the name of beauty, He stamps His image staring back at you and proclaims, "*I. Am. Pleased.*"

How are you responding to the ugly parts in your life?
How is God manifesting Himself in those hollow spaces?

....

....

....

....

....

....

....

....

....

....

....

....

....

....

....

....

....

....

....

Therefore encourage one another and build one another up.

1 THESSALONIANS 5:11 ESV

Before you crawl into bed tonight, whose face do you sense God putting in front of you? Who might be in an uncomfortable season of loss or illness or self-image traps and would benefit from God using you as a palpable megaphone to shout loud, "You are beautiful, and your life is made up of unconditional worth"?

Who could use your encouragement this week? Make a list. Mail a card. Call a friend. Pause and consider how you'll encourage someone daily this week.

....

....

....

....

....

....

....

....

....

....

....

....

....

....

....

....

Draw near to God, and he will draw near to you.

JAMES **4:8** ESV

....
....
....
....
....
....
....
....
....
....
....
....
....
....
....
....
....
....
....
....
....
....
....

Dry is the season of loneliness. But ironically, it's the dry parts that lead to the sweetest understandings. We can't reach the good stuff unless we are willing to be aware that the hard stuff is, in fact, hard. *Isolating.* Maybe solitary isn't something we need to run away from, but an indication to run toward Someone. So it is with noticing my loneliness and recognizing how God is wooing me toward Him.

In times of loneliness, how do you feel God pulling you to Him?

....
....
....
....
....
....
....
....
....
....
....
....
....
....
....
....
....
....
....

" I will never leave you nor forsake you. "

HEBREWS **13:5** ESV

....

....

....

....

....

....

....

....

....

....

....

....

....

....

....

....

....

....

God inches close and says, *"You are never alone. Even if you feel it. I am still here."* And then He reveals whom He places in my path. Our neighbors, the unassuming soul at work, a long-time college friend. *"Do you see who I continually pop in your coming and going? As you go about your life, there they are, showing up just around the bend. Do you see this? They are your hand-picked community."*

Who are "your people"—those whom God has purposefully placed on your path?

....

....

....

....

....

....

....

....

....

....

....

....

....

....

....

....

But by the grace of God I am what I am,
and his grace to me was not without effect.

1 Corinthians 15:10 niv

....
....
....
....
....
....
....
....
....
....
....
....
....
....
....
....
....
....
....
....

Real *is* the new perfect. The kind of authentic-reflecting, where a freeing relationship dwells; where love, joy, peace, patience, and grace abide; where second, third, and fourth chances reside.

How do you embrace #realisthenewperfect when it comes to relationships—primarily your relationship with Jesus?

....

....

....

....

....

....

....

....

....

....

....

....

....

....

....

....

....

....

Where the Spirit of the Lord is, there is freedom.

2 CORINTHIANS 3:17 ESV

As I live in awareness of how truly God relates, how He laughs and I recognize His comic heart, I aspire to reflect genuine laughter like His. As I journey to see His heart smack-dab in the middle of family pictures and social media, I'm inspired to settle into His perfection instead of attempting authenticity on my own.

How can you better reflect your genuine story?

....
....
....
....
....
....
....
....
....
....
....
....
....
....
....
....

In this you rejoice, though now for a little while, if necessary, you have been grieved by various trials, so that the tested genuineness of your faith—more precious than gold that perishes though it is tested by fire—may be found to result in praise and glory and honor at the revelation of Jesus Christ.

1 PETER 1:6–7 ESV

Perfection is found as I follow Jesus into the center of real life—social media included—and come to know His heart, one overflowing with freedom and peace. You want authenticity? Are you craving the genuine of all genuineness? Look no further than within, His dwelling place. Where God, the author of authenticity, the One who actually exists and is not imaginary or fake or artificial, resides.

What distractions do you need to clear away so you can truly see God in the details?

....

....

....

....

....

....

....

....

....

....

....

....

....

....

" And you will know the truth,
and the truth will set you free. "

JOHN **8:32** ESV

A question I ask daily is, *Where am I going for truth?* Truth brings freedom and cements my identity. And truth can come only from the Creator. Am I making time for Him or spending my "free" time online? When I looked back at my involvement online, I noticed feeble attempts for worth strokes and truth teachers. The honest reality? Only Jesus is the Truth—the Author, the Healer, and the Promise of Enough.

How are you embracing Real today?

....

....

....

....

....

....

....

....

....

....

....

....

....

....

....

....

....

But the steadfast love of the LORD is from everlasting to everlasting on those who fear him, and his righteousness to children's children.

PSALM 103:17 ESV

....
....
....
....
....
....
....
....
....
....
....
....
....
....
....
....
....
....
....
....
....
....
....

You know how we model love to our kids? *Time*. We love them with our minutes, hours, and days. We offer Real. We teach them how to use technology as a tool. We step in front of their questions and answer with our faulty experiences and validate what they will wrestle with. We give them permission to crave credibility and remind them that Truth comes not from a tiny device, but from an omnipotent God.

When is it difficult for you to be Real with others?

Let the words of my mouth and the meditation of my heart be acceptable in Your sight.

PSALM 19:14 NKJV

....
....
....
....
....
....
....
....
....
....
....
....
....
....
....
....
....
....
....
....
....
....

If God's first priority is relationships, why not take my hurts and fears and expectations to Him and start with, "Okay, God, this feels really awkward" and let Him speak His thoughts before I react? When I respond with Holy Spirit–saturated words, I'm finding they come from a place of heart connection, not control.

Communicating value begins with asking simple questions: "How do you feel valued?" "How can I best understand your heart in this moment?" What other simple questions might you ask?

....

....

....

....

....

....

....

....

....

....

....

....

....

....

....

....

....

Pleasant words are like a honeycomb,
sweetness to the soul and health to the bones.

PROVERBS 16:24 NKJV

To discern whether expectations are valid or inching too close to an unhealthy ledge, I seek wisdom in the Psalms. "May these words of my mouth and this meditation of my heart be pleasing in your sight, LORD, my Rock and my Redeemer" (19:14 NIV). *God, how I want my words to be a beautiful overflow of my heart condition to You and to those I count dear.*

*What are your expectations in your relationships—
with family, friends, etc.? Are they realistic?*

And my God shall supply all your need according to His riches in glory by Christ Jesus.

PHILIPPIANS 4:19 NKJV

Having needs isn't needy; it's honest. And if my heart yearns to follow after Jesus, I am learning to be confident and vocal in my needs, and then let Him meet me when those expectations aren't met.

How has the Creator met your needs?

*My mouth shall speak wisdom; the meditation
of my heart shall be understanding.*

PSALM 49:3 ESV

Speaking plainly follows Jesus' heart, for in it there are no hidden agendas or passive manipulations. Simply "Let your 'Yes' be 'Yes,' and your 'No,' 'No' " (Matthew 5:37 NKJV).

When it comes to communicating with others,
what do you find to be most challenging?

For you are my rock and my fortress; and for your name's sake you lead me and guide me.

PSALM 31:3 ESV

....
....
....
....
....
....
....
....
....
....
....
....
....
....
....
....
....
....
....
....

God cares about my heart. The more I choose to respond to my discomfort, bring Him my troubles, ask for His advice, and let myself sit with Him in it, the more I find His Spirit gradually provides the answer. If my faith relationship consisted only of God telling me what to do and offering fix-it strategies, I'd feel more like a robot and less like a friend.

When do you forget to show others that you care about their hearts?

One who loves a pure heart and who speaks with grace will have the king for a friend.

PROVERBS 22:11 NIV

I wonder how many relationships can be remedied if I take the time to speak honestly, ask questions, and pray to see hearts.

What is your prayer today for a relationship that needs mending?

*The aim of our charge is love that issues from a
pure heart and a good conscience and a sincere faith.*

1 TIMOTHY 1:5 ESV

Real relationships, *rea*lationships, resemble the heart of the Father with deep layers of openness, asking, sharing, and mostly listening. I won't nail them perfectly on the first try or ever, but I sure do get more comfortable the more I dig in.

How, friend, how do you feel valued?

....

....

....

....

....

....

....

....

....

....

....

....

....

....

....

....

....

....

But godliness with contentment is great gain.

1 TIMOTHY 6:6 NIV

I'm learning that thankfulness comes from a space of trust.
And I can't be thankful when my life is overflowing with excess,
because then I focus on the stuff, instead of the stuff giver.
While contentment reflects a grateful heart, comparison produces
a heart focused on what's lacking instead of what is.

When do you fall into the comparison trap?

....

....

....

....

....

....

....

....

....

....

....

....

....

....

....

....

....

....

....

Give thanks in all circumstances; for this is God's will for you in Christ Jesus.

1 Thessalonians 5:18 NIV

....
....
....
....
....
....
....
....
....
....
....
....
....
....
....
....
....
....
....
....
....
....

My spirit of gratitude comes when I stop looking around and wondering, *When is my life going to get better or become something special?* How ungrateful! What I'm really saying is, "God, this isn't quite good enough for the story I'm wanting."

What are you thankful for today?

....

....

....

....

....

....

....

....

....

....

....

....

....

....

....

....

....

....

And my soul shall be joyful in the LORD;
it shall rejoice in His salvation.

PSALM 35:9 NKJV

....

....

....

....

....

....

....

....

....

....

....

....

....

....

....

....

....

....

Fullness and life and the source of all joy is found in spending time with God, drawing from Him, then reflecting His Son.

What brings you joy?

....

....

....

....

....

....

....

....

....

....

....

....

....

....

....

....

....

....

....

....

....

....

Every good gift and every perfect gift is from above, and comes down from the Father of lights, with whom there is no variation or shadow of turning.

JAMES 1:17 NKJV

God loves giving good gifts to His kids, and He does so in abundance and often. Unfortunately, we often don't see them because we are looking for them in the wrong places—in the past or the future—instead of smack-dab in front of us.

Have you been focused on the past or future instead of the present? If so, what good gifts might you have been missing?

....

....

....

....

....

....

....

....

....

....

....

....

....

....

....

....

....

Let the word of Christ dwell in you richly,
teaching and admonishing one another in all wisdom,
singing psalms and hymns and spiritual songs,
with thankfulness in your hearts to God.

COLOSSIANS 3:16 ESV

If everything I want comes my direction, I'll never have to learn how to be grateful, because gratitude is learned by being thankful for what is, not obsessing over what is not. Until I am satisfied with the Giver, all the pillows and couches and lip gloss bouquets in the world won't create an appreciative spirit.

In what areas do you find yourself obsessing over what isn't rather than what is?

Blessed are the people whose God is the LORD!

PSALM 144:15 ESV

God loves me and wants me to be content in Him, with Him. With that understanding comes a renewed awareness, for *I. am. blessed.* Every good thing comes from Him.

In what ways has God blessed you? Write them down and spend a moment rejoicing and thanking Him.

Rejoice always, pray continually, give thanks in all circumstances; for this is God's will for you in Christ Jesus.

1 THESSALONIANS 5:16–18 NIV

....
....
....
....
....
....
....
....
....
....
....
....
....
....
....
....
....
....
....
....
....
....
....
....

I believe God smiles when we take the time to sit in His presence and thank Him for doing life with us. I believe the angels lend an ear when we gather in groups and communally give thanks.

What is your prayer of thanksgiving today?

Praise the LORD! Praise God in his sanctuary; praise him in his mighty heavens! Praise him for his mighty deeds; praise him according to his excellent greatness! Praise him with trumpet sound; praise him with lute and harp!

PSALM 150:1–3 ESV

_____

_____

_____

_____

_____

_____

_____

_____

_____

_____

_____

_____

_____

_____

_____

_____

God cares about encouraging His children to live joyfully and fully and with thanksgiving on their tongues. When we choose appreciative awareness for the small things, we live contentedly and are quick to praise for the big things.

What "small things" do you appreciate the most?

....

....

....

....

....

....

....

....

....

....

....

....

....

....

....

....

....

....

Give ear and hear my voice, listen and hear my speech.

ISAIAH **28:23** NKJV

_____
_____
_____
_____
_____
_____
_____
_____
_____
_____
_____
_____
_____
_____
_____
_____
_____
_____
_____
_____
_____
_____

What do these three tasks—praying, rejoicing, and giving thanks—have in common? They are all something we offer back to God, part of our ongoing conversation—a continuous listen and share, and share and listen relationship—as He so generously places His will in our laps.

When you share with God, how do you also
slow down and really listen for His response?

....

....

....

....

....

....

....

....

....

....

....

....

....

....

....

....

....

....

. . .that the genuineness of your faith, being much more precious than gold that perishes, though it is tested by fire, may be found to praise, honor, and glory at the revelation of Jesus Christ.

1 PETER 1:7 NKJV

There's nothing genuine about artificial thanks. If my nearest and dearest can spot my phoniness, why do I think I can fool God? He wants my praise, but He wants the real kind. When I see His heart in whatever the day holds, believe it's His best for me, and respond with gratitude—that, I'm learning, is true thanksgiving.

When do you find yourself offering God disingenuous praise? What prompts this? How can you cultivate a spirit of genuine gratitude?

And we know that all things work together for good to those who love God, to those who are the called according to His purpose.

ROMANS 8:28 NKJV

There will be good and bad; I will give praise for it, and God will be glorified in it. Even when shrouded in smoke. . .being thankful is a choice, and living gratefully, a natural response to a full, appreciative heart.

What hinders you from living gratefully?

....

....

....

....

....

....

....

....

....

....

....

....

....

....

....

....

....

....

Who created all these? He who brings out the starry host one by one and calls forth each of them by name. Because of his great power and mighty strength, not one of them is missing.

ISAIAH **40:26** NIV

When I respond to a moment, like my boys waving for me to watch
a family of ducks play in the wash below, cupping it carefully with
awe, I can better see God's fingerprints on it. For up close is
where I notice details. The creativity. The invitation to thank
the Maker for blowing my mind with a confetti of gifts.

What "confetti of gifts" has the Maker rained down on you?

....

....

....

....

....

....

....

....

....

....

....

....

....

....

....

That person is like a tree planted by streams of water, which yields its fruit in season and whose leaf does not wither—whatever they do prospers.

PSALM 1:3 NIV

I'm not sure thanks is authentic if offered when life mainly sails smooth. Being thankful shouldn't be my pathetic cry to avoid hardships. Real gratitude says thank you when winter comes and leaves are blown and you're standing bare and cold and vulnerable and even while shaking, commit: "I am thankful in all circumstances and will celebrate nonetheless."

How can we celebrate a genuine faith relationship if we don't give thanks in the bare seasons as well as in the abundant ones?

O LORD my God, in you do I take refuge.

PSALM 7:1 ESV

....
....
....
....
....
....
....
....
....
....
....
....
....
....
....
....
....
....
....
....
....
....

When I choose to celebrate God's goodness *always*, *continually*, and *in all circumstances*, gratitude is embodied, even if blocked by ashy smoke or cut down by bare branches. Will I utter thanks before the debris clears and the leaves grow back? Anticipating Real as the source? Of light. Of strength. Of a safe place to find warmth and shade.

How is God's Spirit inviting you to practice gratitude?

....

....

....

....

....

....

....

....

....

....

....

....

....

....

....

....

....

Ascribe to the LORD the glory due his name;
worship the LORD in the splendor of his holiness.

PSALM 29:2 NIV

GODsense changes my perspective from once living as though sensory situations happened *to me* to now living *into* senses, gobbling each one up as a willing, all-in participant. With a tilt-my-head-back eagerness to embrace however God is offering Himself. For there is sacred work in noticing. In offering attention to everyday details and, once exposed, craving them in never-before ways with an all-sensory appetite for smells, sights, sounds, tastes, and textures.

How have you experienced GODsense—a sudden appreciation and insatiable desire to see, taste, smell, hear, and feel Him in every moment of every day?

Great is our Lord and mighty in power;
his understanding has no limit.

PSALM 147:5 NIV

God gets it. He knows me. And He knows you. He knows what's going on in our lives, and He is meeting us exactly where we are in such personal, out-of-the-box displays.

How does it feel to know that God gets it, that He understands what you're going through in life?

....

....

....

....

....

....

....

....

....

....

....

....

....

....

....

....

....

....

O LORD, our Lord, How excellent is Your name in all the earth, Who have set Your glory above the heavens!

PSALM 8:1 NKJV

Once you experience God's Spirit inviting you to notice and respond and celebrate Him in all of life's fullness, you can't ignore how Real He is.

How do you experience God in the wonders of His creation?

. . . .

. . . .

. . . .

. . . .

. . . .

. . . .

. . . .

. . . .

. . . .

. . . .

. . . .

. . . .

. . . .

. . . .

. . . .

. . . .

. . . .

"Call to me and I will answer you and tell you great and unsearchable things you do not know."

JEREMIAH 33:3 NIV

....
....
....
....
....
....
....
....
....
....
....
....
....
....
....
....
....
....
....
....
....
....

I'm discovering how gentle Jesus is. Not a yeller, He whispers in the waves, breezes, rain. Before my senses were awakened, I'd ask, "What does God's voice sound like?" Now I pause, attune my ears, and there He is.

Where and when did you last hear God's voice?

"The Spirit gives life; the flesh counts for nothing. The words I have spoken to you—they are full of the Spirit and life."

JOHN 6:63 NIV

Why do I expect the Almighty to talk in a low rumble when He
is not confined to words alone but uses the sea and seagulls
and sand to echo His presence through crashes, cries,
and crunching underfoot? The question isn't "What does His
voice sound like?" but "Am I creating space to hear Him?"

How are you creating space to hear the Almighty speak?

....

....

....

....

....

....

....

....

....

....

....

....

....

....

....

....

....

....

"Before they call I will answer; while they are still speaking I will hear."

ISAIAH **65:24** NIV

....
....
....
....
....
....
....
....
....
....
....
....
....
....
....
....
....
....
....
....
....
....

Do you also wonder about what God's voice sounds like?
Have you prayed to hear Him? In a worship song? A family jingle?
A beach walk? The voice of His Spirit on how to parent your child?
He will answer when you ask. And most likely it will be more
amazing and unexpected than ordinary words.

When did God offer an answer before
you even asked for His perspective?

For we are to God the fragrance of Christ among those who are being saved and among those who are perishing.

2 Corinthians 2:15 NKJV

In creating our senses, God spared no details, and with smell, He went above and beyond. When He could simply dip roses in clouds and fling them through sunsets, He didn't pause there but poured fragrant perfume on each petal.

What good memories do you associate with the sense of smell? Jot them down and relish these GODsense moments.

....

....

....

....

....

....

....

....

....

....

....

....

....

....

....

....

....

And walk in love, as Christ loved us and gave himself up for us, a fragrant offering and sacrifice to God.

EPHESIANS 5:2 ESV

How can we experience a spiritual moment with our senses?
Beyond simply smelling—how can we find deeper faith through a
God who wants to connect with us through perfume or herbs?

What smells carry stories from a distinct moment in time?

....

....

....

....

....

....

....

....

....

....

....

....

....

....

....

....

....

....

But it is good for me to draw near to God.

PSALM 73:28 NKJV

By noticing delicate fragrances of flowers, ocean air scents, and perfume, I glimpse a window into how our Father must smell, as I make myself at home by His side or in His lap. How rich to breathe in the smells surrounding our days and invite my kids to recognize Him with their own sniffers. *Do you smell that? It's the smell of the Father.*

What is your favorite scent and why?

....

....

....

....

....

....

....

....

....

....

....

....

....

....

....

....

"You, LORD, in the beginning laid the foundation of the earth, and the heavens are the work of Your hands."

HEBREWS 1:10 NKJV

....
....
....
....
....
....
....
....
....
....
....
....
....
....
....
....
....
....
....

God takes utter delight in inviting us to feel alive with colors, tastes, goose bumps, sounds, and aromas that offer dimension to the otherwise dreary. What if GODsense is a gift for average hours and real-life circumstances, an engaging way to pull back the earthly curtain and celebrate a foretaste of heaven?

What do you imagine heaven will be like?

....
....
....
....
....
....
....
....
....
....
....
....
....
....
....
....
....

Rejoice in the Lord always. Again I will say, rejoice!

PHILIPPIANS 4:4 NKJV

....

....

....

....

....

....

....

....

....

....

....

....

....

....

....

....

....

....

....

....

....

....

....

When we take average moments like preparing, eating, and cleaning up meals, and layer them with songs and swaying, we celebrate the ordinary. *Why celebrate?* For no other reason than it's a random Wednesday evening, and we can either wish it toward Friday or choose to make memories out of the average ho-hum of a hump day.

How will you choose to celebrate the ordinary?

....

....

....

....

....

....

....

....

....

....

....

....

....

....

....

....

....

....

Be glad in the LORD and rejoice, you righteous;
and shout for joy, all you upright in heart!

PSALM 32:11 NKJV

....
....
....
....
....
....
....
....
....
....
....
....
....
....
....
....
....
....
....

Where do most of us spend 90 percent of our time? On our very normal couch, in our average home, eating off everyday dishes, cleaning up after dogs that poop, and creating intentionally safe space where disagreements and laughter and chaos occur. Normal rhythms begging us to see Jesus as Real. The everyday is not like a shiny musical, friend, where the best version is highlighted with glitz and lights. It's life, and honoring it is a choice.

What do you love most about your "normal" routine?

He calms the storm.

PSALM 107:29 NKJV

When the *tick-tock* of an envisioned routine becomes my god, when life ignores my precious memo and steals my dependent focus, when I lose all desire to dance in the average, I take up a critical dance, a complaining waltz. The anxious pounding of my heart drowns out my choosing to see God in the storm. And if I'm honest, more days bring unexpected drops than perfectly planned mists. My response in the ordinary builds perseverance for the torrential downpours, creating space for deep faith.

How has God met you in the storm?

....

....

....

....

....

....

....

....

....

....

....

....

....

....

....

....

You are my hiding place; you will protect me from trouble and surround me with songs of deliverance.

PSALM 32:7 NIV

....
....
....
....
....
....
....
....
....
....
....
....
....
....
....
....
....
....
....
....

Why is it I feel as if grander experiences equate to an epic faith?
Isn't it, in fact, the other way around? The deep dependency,
the down-in-the-mess, Jesus-clinging experiences like loss and
pain and rejection make for a more robust relationship.

What words would you use to describe your relationship with Jesus?

....

....

....

....

....

....

....

....

....

....

....

....

....

....

....

....

....

....

A faithful person will be richly blessed.

PROVERBS **28:20** NIV

....
....
....
....
....
....
....
....
....
....
....
....
....
....
....
....
....
....
....
....
....
....
....

The higher the mountain doesn't mean the closer to God. It's in the average details of today that we get to put our faith into practice. And when I find myself hoping to trade in for bigger and better, including our house, our lifestyle, our (*ahem*) kiddos, I hold tight to where I spend the majority of my time—in the average, where the ordinary is epically best.

When do you feel closest to God?

....

....

....

....

....

....

....

....

....

....

....

....

....

....

....

....

But for me it is good to be near God.

Psalm 73:28 ESV

. . . .

. . . .

. . . .

. . . .

. . . .

. . . .

. . . .

. . . .

. . . .

. . . .

. . . .

. . . .

. . . .

. . . .

. . . .

. . . .

. . . .

. . . .

. . . .

. . . .

Let's live our lives on purpose, shall we? Be it in flooded floors, playing in the sandbox, or waiting in line at the DMV, count me in, however unplanned detours direct us. God meets us in the simplest of moments and transforms our minds to view our schedules, work, parenting, and responsibilities as a way to dance in the storm.

When did you last notice God's presence in a simple, everyday moment?

....

....

....

....

....

....

....

....

....

....

....

....

....

....

....

....

"But now, Lord, what do I look for? My hope is in you."
PSALM 39:7 NIV

....
....
....
....
....
....
....
....
....
....
....
....
....
....
....
....
....
....
....
....
....
....

Nothing, my friend, is wasted. God is using every drop—whether from rain or tears or sparkly paper thrown in celebration—to urge us to keep going, keep giving, keep living in today. Keep pushing against the social norms, the false expectations, the racing against the clock to achieve, arrive, and get there. There is no *there*. There is only *here*.

How are you enjoying the here and now?

....

....

....

....

....

....

....

....

....

....

....

....

....

....

....

....

*"I have come that they may have life,
and have it to the full."*

JOHN 10:10 NIV

....
....
....
....
....
....
....
....
....
....
....
....
....
....
....
....
....
....
....
....
....
....
....
....
....

The tension between wanting perfection or wanting to experience "this right here," will always exist. When I hold up a mirror to what today holds, a million choices reflect back. How will I respond? Will it be life-gulping or self-gratifying? Wouldn't you rather dance through the routine than resent, criticize, complain, escape, or abhor it? Isn't it the reality that most of our days *are* spent in the average: working, cooking, cleaning, parenting, coaching, and sometimes just plain surviving?

How do you balance the pull between wanting perfection and wanting to experience the "right here and now" moment?

....

....

....

....

....

....

....

....

....

....

....

....

....

....

....

*Many are the plans in a person's heart,
but it is the LORD's purpose that prevails.*

PROVERBS 19:21 NIV

At the root of believing that *epicness equals value* is the core fear that my story is not epic and therefore lacks purpose. If I pad my self-worth with grand vacations and life-changing prayer nights and, on the rare occasion, incredible parenting moments, those circumstances will distract from the reality that my story is ever so simple.

When do you feel this way—that your story needs to be huge and spotlighty and world changing in order to matter? That somehow God can't use you just as you are, where you are?

....

....

....

....

....

....

....

....

....

....

....

....

....

....

....

....

The whole earth is filled with awe at your wonders;
where morning dawns, where evening fades,
you call forth songs of joy.

PSALM 65:8 NIV

....
....
....
....
....
....
....
....
....
....
....
....
....
....
....
....
....
....
....
....
....
....

Epicness, I'm finding, is an unobtainable expectation, a dream I've created in my head that suffocates sincere joy. When I put down contentment and pick up the lie that *wow* moments hold the most value, I resent reality. Reality, however, brings freedom when I recognize that epic is our everyday.

How would you describe an epic life?

....

....

....

....

....

....

....

....

....

....

....

....

....

....

....

....

....

I have learned to be content whatever the circumstances.

PHILIPPIANS 4:11 NIV

Epic is celebrating my story. And epic is celebrating your story.
And it doesn't depend on the level of grandness or cost,
but in how content we are with our everyday lives.

In what areas are you content? Discontent?
Explore why for the next few minutes.

You need to persevere so that when you have done the will of God, you will receive what he has promised.

HEBREWS **10:36** NIV

Today will most likely overflow with ordinary moments. What it won't hold is another chance to celebrate it, to dance *into* its fabulous averageness, to grab your babes and whisk them around the kitchen, to look into the eyes of a spouse who knows you through and through and whisper, "I'd choose you again. Even when it's hard." To pay bills and scramble eggs and pick up dog poop, knowing today will never come again, and by welcoming what comes, to applaud perseverance.

Are you a "welcome what comes" kind of person? Why or why not?

....

....

....

....

....

....

....

....

....

....

....

....

....

....

....

....

*. . .that we may lead a quiet and peaceable
life in all godliness and reverence.*

1 Timothy 2:2 NKJV

How do we honor the microscopic details of today? How do we experience God as real in the routine? We choose them. Deliberately. With consideration and reverence.

Write a prayer of thanksgiving. Leave your prayer in a visible place and read it daily.

This is what I have observed to be good: that it is appropriate for a person to eat, to drink and to find satisfaction in their toilsome labor under the sun during the few days of life God has given them—for this is their lot.

ECCLESIASTES 5:18 NIV

....
....
....
....
....
....
....
....
....
....
....
....
....
....
....
....
....
....
....

Savoring the ho-hum of the everyday, even when it feels like tedious work, adds lively steps and beautiful lyrics, a connecting rhythm overlapping with stories, faces, and dance parties that are missed if not engaged in and enjoyed. Today? It's quite epic, indeed.

How will you choose to fully engage in the moments of today?

....

....

....

....

....

....

....

....

....

....

....

....

....

....

....

....

....

....

For no one is cast off by the Lord forever. Though he brings grief, he will show compassion, so great is his unfailing love. For he does not willingly bring affliction or grief to anyone.

LAMENTATIONS 3:31–33 NIV

....
....
....
....
....
....
....
....
....
....
....
....
....
....
....
....
....
....
....
....
....

Giving of ourselves in the wake of grief is perhaps the next closest spiritual act to touching God Himself. We are made bitter or better because of our circumstances.

How might difficult circumstances make a person better?

....

....

....

....

....

....

....

....

....

....

....

....

....

....

....

....

....

....

....

Therefore if you have any encouragement from being united with Christ, if any comfort from his love, if any common sharing in the Spirit, if any tenderness and compassion, then make my joy complete by being like-minded, having the same love, being one in spirit and of one mind. Do nothing out of selfish ambition or vain conceit. Rather, in humility value others above yourselves, not looking to your own interests but each of you to the interests of the others.

PHILIPPIANS 2:1–4 NIV

When we make a decision to use our pain by taking the focus off ourselves and placing it with passionate perspective on another, faith is planted deeply in the fertile soil of knowing loss. When this selfless behavior becomes a habit, blooms are plucked from strong branches and given away as bouquets to thankful souls.

How can you use the gifts you are given right where you are to be Jesus' hands and feet to those who need care the most?

A generous person will prosper;
whoever refreshes others will be refreshed.

PROVERBS 11:25 NIV

Turning outward is fueled by our hardest days, when we let go of controlled plans and reach beyond ourselves with a desire to reflect Real. But when the blues invite, isn't it easy to wallow in our stuckness? We map out our lives, knowing how they ought to unfurl, but when details go awry, do we focus on the rearranged aspects or on how God is using the detours to bring our attention to people rather than to our goals?

How has God used a detour in your life to do something wonderful?

We ought always to thank God for you, brothers and sisters, and rightly so, because your faith is growing more and more, and the love all of you have for one another is increasing.

2 THESSALONIANS 1:3 NIV

....
....
....
....
....
....
....
....
....
....
....
....
....
....
....
....
....

Sometimes we just want to throw the covers over our heads and chalk our blues up to "one of those days," and for those occasions, friend, there's grace. But after a while, if we allow the blues to become our identity, we are stunted, not grown, by hardship. Challenges—however they come—must be journeyed through in order to experience healing, removing the focus from ourselves and putting it on others.

What do you find most difficult about focusing on others when you're in the middle of a personal challenge?

....

....

....

....

....

....

....

....

....

....

....

....

....

....

....

We may be mutually encouraged by each other's faith, both yours and mine.

ROMANS 1:12 ESV

....
....
....
....
....
....
....
....
....
....
....
....
....
....
....
....
....
....
....
....

When I use my own story to come alongside hurting souls, relatability and compassion and the sacred art of giving are born. Navigating hardship is like trudging through deep, sticky mud. Underneath, movement is taking place, but it often feels like millimeter-ish, heavy, slow-motion steps. The truth is, journeying forward is a process—a messy one at that—and when I pull from my own pain story to meet yours, my focus no longer lingers on my affliction but on the opportunity to put tangible meat and potatoes to Jesus' words: "It is more blessed to give than to receive" (Acts 20:35 ESV).

*How do you feel when you come alongside
and lift up someone who is hurting?*

"Let your light shine before others, so that they may see your good works and give glory to your Father who is in heaven."

MATTHEW 5:16 ESV

When dim circumstances surround, it's as if the light we carry is stifled within, snuffed out; it only smokes and chokes and clouds clarity, causing further suffering. But when we take our light, even with a shaky hand, and share it with another, we turn our pain inside out; and in doing so, compassion and a spirit of sacrifice are born.

How can you share your light with others?

....

....

....

....

....

....

....

....

....

....

....

....

....

....

....

....

....

That is why, for Christ's sake, I delight in weaknesses, in insults, in hardships, in persecutions, in difficulties. For when I am weak, then I am strong.

2 CORINTHIANS 12:10 NIV

I'm asked to choose on a daily basis whether I'll succumb to my circumstances or turn my feelings outward and be available to how God wants to use my imperfect situation. Some days I stay put in my stinky funk, allowing smoke to swirl and choke any love that God wants to pull out and pass on. On other days I respond to His Spirit's nudge and come alongside someone else who is holding the same concern, and whisper, "God's not going to waste your pain. He's going to use it in beautiful ways. And if you can't see it now, that's okay. I'm here as His mouthpiece to say, 'You are seen. Where you are today is noticed. I'm affirming your process.' "

How do you feel lighter and more hopeful on days when you follow God's nudge to have an outward focus?

Be devoted to one another in love.
Honor one another above yourselves.

ROMANS 12:10 NIV

When I step out of my comfort zone to assure another hurting soul that she is not alone, I am ministering healing in the form of love. Where before I thought serving was essential to feel better, I now understand that it's not about giving with the motive of trying to make my icky feelings go away, but to use my discomfort as a catalyst for compassion. To come alongside and say, "I get it. I'm in the thick of it too. Let's journey this together for today."

How do you feel when someone else says,
"I get it. Let's journey together"?

....

....

....

....

....

....

....

....

....

....

....

....

....

....

....

"It is more blessed to give than to receive."

ACTS 20:35 NIV

....
....
....
....
....
....
....
....
....
....
....
....
....
....
....
....
....
....

Turning outward encompasses everything God is about: relationships. Intimate, Father-known, Jesus-dependent, Spirit-saturated-type relationships. Relationships that involve giving and receiving and then giving again, from a space of being known and enough. He gives. We receive. Then we give. Turning outward is like putting on "selfless" glasses. It doesn't change how the situation looks, but it does shift the perspective from me to Him to others.

What does turning outward look like for you?

The LORD is good to all; he has compassion on all he has made.

PSALM 145:9 NIV

I'm convinced God meets us, knows us, and offers a dependent relationship in our pain, but He doesn't let us stay there. He uses our suffering to encourage and relate when others need comfort. He doesn't ask us to give so others will make us feel better, but as an invitation to choose to walk alongside a hurting soul. Perhaps compassionate pain is where healing begins.

How has compassion been healing for you?

Rejoice with those who rejoice;
mourn with those who mourn.

ROMANS 12:15 NIV

Like a magnet, when Jesus is at the center of your pain, do you find yourself drawn to the knowing arms of others who have survived the process of peeling back raw grief layers? We get it. We are an afflicted crew, you and me. There is something deep and powerful about linking arms and, as an imperfect community, turning ourselves inside out so others can better relate to our messy insides.

Who can you link arms with today?

Having gifts that differ according to the grace given to us, let us use them.

ROMANS 12:6 ESV

....
....
....
....
....
....
....
....
....
....
....
....
....
....
....
....
....
....
....
....
....

A bunch of marks and dents and dings come with the territory of living, but what if we respond with outward thinking and, on our worst days, walk into a room and see just one soul and give? Give of our encouragement and applause. Give of our time and priorities. Give of our energy and the truth that today is so much more joy-filled when we make it less about our self-focused needs and more about God's selfless relationship.

How will you choose to look outward and give of yourself today?

....

....

....

....

....

....

....

....

....

....

....

....

....

....

....

....

Light dawns in the darkness for the upright.

PSALM 112:4 ESV

....
....
....
....
....
....
....
....
....
....
....
....
....
....
....
....
....
....
....
....
....
....

How are you using your light in the dark? Where are you choosing to illuminate how God is authentic and present and working? Even in your frustrations, pains, and disappointments? In your grief and "just because" funks? How are you choosing Real?

Where do you naturally use your talents and gifts? How can you pour your passion into someone when the hard days come?

....

....

....

....

....

....

....

....

....

....

....

....

....

....

....

....

....

....

*Faithfulness springs up from the ground,
and righteousness looks down from the sky.*

PSALM **85:11** ESV

Living outward is a result of focusing upward. Turning outward starts with prayer, a conversation of listening and doing. Of noting how our faith perspective grows bigger than our agenda when we ask God, "How do You want to use my situation as part of Your massive plan?"

What brings life from your fingertips?
How can you share your joy with another soul?

....

....

....

....

....

....

....

....

....

....

....

....

....

....

....

....

Blessed are all who fear the LORD,
who walk in obedience to him.

PSALM 128:1 NIV

What can I do? How can I use my skills to help others, you ask? Simple. Start where you are with the gifts you have. Do you feel alive speaking? Painting? Designing? Opening your home and putting out brownies and helping people experience a sense of belonging? Your ministry doesn't have to start big or become monumental; your God-given purpose may start with a prompting of His Spirit and a willingness to be present, to be obedient, to offer joy when you want to sulk.

What are your gifts and passions?

....

....

....

....

....

....

....

....

....

....

....

....

....

....

....

....

The unfolding of your words gives light.

PSALM 119:130 NIV

Don't allow others' success to diminish the story God is prompting for your journey. Don't miss out on the gifts He uniquely shines through you. Don't squelch the light He desires to burst forth from you so that others can know Him. Because God's love, friends, is never self-serving.

When do you notice yourself getting in the way of God's desires for you?

....

....

....

....

....

....

....

....

....

....

....

....

....

....

....

....

Never be lacking in zeal, but keep your spiritual fervor, serving the Lord.

ROMANS 12:11 NIV

....
....
....
....
....
....
....
....
....
....
....
....
....
....
....
....
....
....
....
....
....

What if God is using your fervor as means for someone else to find a relationship with the Divine? What if bad days aren't part of our plan but we can use them to point back to Someone who is sovereign? What if we can use uncomfortable situations to teach our children to be aware of others, even when they are afraid or lonely or sad themselves? What if the simple choice in offering our eyes, our ears, and our hands to see, listen, and comfort is not about what we can give but about being changed because we have received from God first?

How will you choose to use your gifts today?

....

....

....

....

....

....

....

....

....

....

....

....

....

....

....

For the sake of my family and friends,
I will say, "Peace be within you."

PSALM 122:8 NIV

....
....
....
....
....
....
....
....
....
....
....
....
....
....
....
....
....
....
....
....
....
....

When we stop obsessing over ourselves and adopt a selfless perspective, we notice how everyone has pain marks that need to be validated and comforted. Turning outward brings peace to anxious souls and smiles at plans gone haywire.

How can you better gain a selfless perspective?

I know that there is nothing better for people than to be happy and to do good while they live.

ECCLESIASTES 3:12 NIV

A pivotal part of experiencing the act of turning outward is offering the gift of celebrating someone else, even in our own imperfect circumstances. And that reminds us to continue looking out and beyond and up.

Is it easy to celebrate someone else when your own life isn't going quite like you'd hoped? Why or why not?

....

....

....

....

....

....

....

....

....

....

....

....

....

....

....

....

....

There is no fear in love. But perfect love drives out fear, because fear has to do with punishment. The one who fears is not made perfect in love.

1 JOHN 4:18 NIV

....
....
....
....
....
....
....
....
....
....
....
....
....
....
....
....
....
....
....

The enemy doesn't want me to be confident and live from the truth that I'm loved no matter what. And he sure doesn't want me to remind you of the same: that the God who created the stunning ocean and stellar universe loves *you* unconditionally. Nope, the ugly deceiver wants all of us to keep going around on the same crazy cycle believing we are weird. Sorry, Satan, you lose.

When do you find it difficult to tune out the lies of the enemy?

Whatever is true, whatever is noble, whatever is right, whatever is pure, whatever is lovely, whatever is admirable—if anything is excellent or praiseworthy—think about such things.

PHILIPPIANS **4:8** NIV

Our minds are like empty rooms to fill with the thoughts we choose, the very thoughts that create or destroy a safe abode. Here's the catch. Every thought follows a choice: *Do you want truth or lies inside that noggin?* I imagine decorating my mind with focused thoughts designed alongside Philippians 4:8.

How can you focus your mind on God's precious truth?

....

....

....

....

....

....

....

....

....

....

....

....

....

....

....

....

....

Search me, God, and know my heart;
test me and know my anxious thoughts.

PSALM 139:23 NIV

....
....
....
....
....
....
....
....
....
....
....
....
....
....
....
....
....
....
....
....

We are not victims but permission-givers of our thoughts. Remember?
We choose which thoughts stay and which lies take a hike. I spend extra
time where I'm most reminded of God's unfailing adoration, which usually
is in nature, or with people, not in situations where fear readily lurks.
By claiming, not questioning God's love, the fullness of life is
experienced. And friend, we can't live fully if we are afraid.

How will you claim God's love today?

....

....

....

....

....

....

....

....

....

....

....

....

....

....

....

....

....

....

*For God so loved the world that he gave his one and only Son,
that whoever believes in him shall not perish but have eternal life.*

JOHN 3:16 NIV

....
....
....
....
....
....
....
....
....
....
....
....
....
....
....
....
....
....
....
....
....
....
....
....
....

YOU matter is a daily party God throws, one where He presents glittery party sparklers, supplies the matches, and extends to us the fun task of running and planting them in unexpected hands, only to enjoy watching, once lit, fiery and gold, His love reflected in their glowing smiles.

Whose sparkler will you light today?

....

....

....

....

....

....

....

....

....

....

....

....

....

....

....

....

....

....

....

We love because [Christ] first loved us.

1 JOHN 4:19 NIV

YOU matter is simply an invitation to celebrate everyone, because when you believe you are loved, you are amped to uplift others who desperately need to be seen and known and encouraged. *YOU matter* is using tangible hands and feet to validate, jump in, and assure the truth of 1 John 4:19.

How can you share the message "YOU matter"
with someone who needs to hear it this week?

....

....

....

....

....

....

....

....

....

....

....

....

....

....

....

....

. . .that I may be encouraged together with you by the mutual faith both of you and me.

ROMANS 1:12 NKJV

YOU matter is championing those who are interested in the same things you are, those who are possibly further ahead or more noticed or more successful, and genuinely telling them, "You are doing a fabulous job. Thank you for letting your light shine. Keep going."

How will you reach out and choose to champion someone's efforts today?

....

....

....

....

....

....

....

....

....

....

....

....

....

....

....

....

....

....

"If you greet only your own people, what are you doing more than others? Do not even pagans do that?"

MATTHEW 5:47 NIV

....
....
....
....
....
....
....
....
....
....
....
....
....
....
....
....
....
....
....
....

By extending God's hand in the form of yours, looking into someone's eyes, and saying, "I see you. I am for you. And YOU matter," love breathes new life. By offering unconditional love, you are receiving the freeing gift of giving God's love away, trusting His Spirit will show up in even bigger expressions.

How is sharing God's love freeing for you?

....

....

....

....

....

....

....

....

....

....

....

....

....

....

....

....

....

For You, Lord, are good, and ready to forgive,
and abundant in mercy to all those who call upon You.

PSALM 86:5 NKJV

I'm learning to cheer others' wins, to cry with others' losses, to turn grief outward, to embrace the scattered steps He places before me, and instead of saying, "God bless my soul, life is so easy and God is so good," I laugh, and with honesty, utter, "This is so not how I thought faith would look, but God's path proves more spontaneous and life giving, more inner-healing abundant than anything I was creating on my own."

How can you best celebrate and enjoy the moments when life doesn't go as planned?

....

....

....

....

....

....

....

....

....

....

....

....

....

....

Read the Devotional that Inspired this Journal!

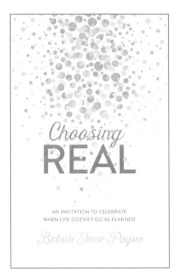

Choosing REAL

by Bekah Jane Pogue

In *Choosing REAL*, author Bekah Pogue walks with women into life's unplanned circumstances—specifically frantic schedules, pain and transition, feelings of unworthiness, loneliness, and tension. And she reminds them it is in these very moments that God invites us to notice, respond, and even *celebrate* how He shows up—in every little detail.

Paperback / 978-1-63409-964-6 / $14.99